THE LITTLE BOOK OF
SELF-CARE
— FOR —
CANCER

*Simple Ways to Refresh
and Restore—According
to the Stars*

CONSTANCE STELLAS

ADAMS MEDIA

NEW YORK · LONDON · TORONTO · SYDNEY · NEW DELHI

Adams Media
An Imprint of Simon & Schuster, Inc.
57 Littlefield Street
Avon, Massachusetts 02322

First Adams Media hardcover edition January 2019

ADAMS MEDIA and colophon are trademarks of Simon & Schuster.

For information about special discounts for bulk purchases, please contact Simon & Schuster Special Sales at 1-866-506-1949 or business@simonandschuster.com.

The Simon & Schuster Speakers Bureau can bring authors to your live event. For more information or to book an event contact the Simon & Schuster Speakers Bureau at 1-866-248-3049 or visit our website at www.simonspeakers.com.

Interior design by Colleen Cunningham
Interior images © Getty Images; Clipart.com

Manufactured in the United States of America

10 9 8 7 6 5 4 3 2 1

Library of Congress Cataloging-in-Publication Data has been applied for.

ISBN 978-1-5072-0970-7
ISBN 978-1-5072-0971-4 (ebook)

Dedication

To my family-loving Cancerian father and husband.

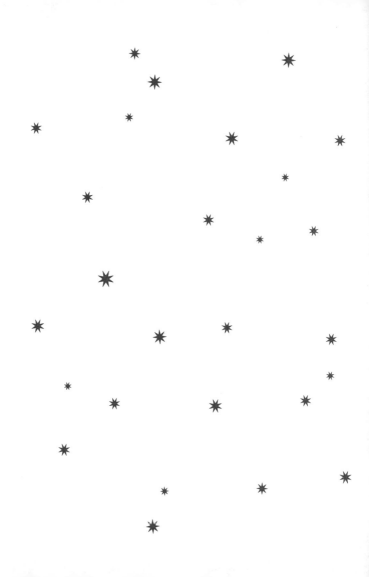

CONTENTS

Introduction   7

PART 1
Signs, Elements, and Self-Care   9

What Is Self-Care?   10

Self-Care and Astrology   17

Essential Elements: Water   24

Self-Care for Cancer   30

PART 2
Self-Care Rituals for Cancer   37

Acknowledgments

I would like to thank Karen Cooper and everyone at Adams Media who helped with this book. To Brendan O'Neill, Katie Corcoran Lytle, Sarah Doughty, Eileen Mullan, Casey Ebert, Sylvia Davis, and everyone else who worked on the manuscripts. To Frank Rivera, Colleen Cunningham, and Katrina Machado for their work on the book's cover and interior design. I appreciated your team spirit and eagerness to dive into the riches of astrology.

Introduction

It's time for you to have a little *"me" time*—powered by the zodiac. By tapping into your Sun sign's astrological and elemental energies, *The Little Book of Self-Care for Cancer* brings star-powered strength and cosmic relief to your life with self-care guidance tailored specifically for you.

While you may enjoy putting others first, Cancer, this book focuses on your true self. This book provides information on how to incorporate self-care into your life while teaching you just how important astrology is to your overall self-care routine. You'll learn more about yourself as you learn about your sign and its governing element, water. Then you can relax, rejuvenate, and stay balanced with more than one hundred self-care ideas and activities perfect for your watery Cancer personality.

From having a past-life reading to getting lost in a great book, you will find plenty of ways to heal your mind, body, and active spirit. Now, let the stars be your self-care guide!

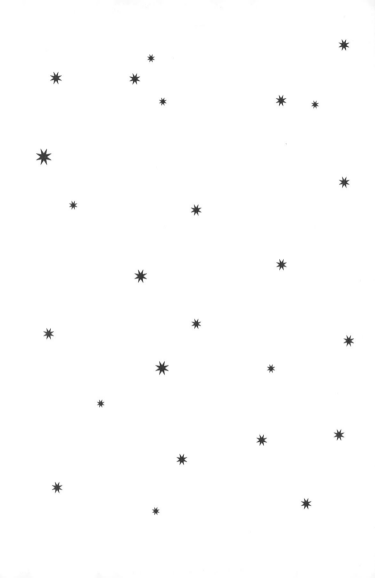

♋

PART 1

SIGNS,
ELEMENTS,
AND
SELF-CARE

CHAPTER 1

WHAT IS SELF-CARE?

✳

Astrology gives insights into whom to love, when to charge forward into new beginnings, and how to succeed in whatever you put your mind to. When paired with self-care, astrology can also help you relax and reclaim that part of yourself that tends to get lost in the bustle of the day. In this chapter you'll learn what self-care is—for you. (No matter your sign, self-care is more than just lit candles and quiet reflection, though these activities may certainly help you find the renewal that you seek.) You'll also learn how making a priority of personalized self-care activities can benefit you in ways you may not even have thought of. Whether you're a Leo, a Pisces, or a Taurus, you deserve rejuvenation and renewal that's customized to your sign—this chapter reveals where to begin.

What Self-Care Is

Self-care is any activity that you do to take care of yourself. It rejuvenates your body, refreshes your mind, or realigns your spirit. It relaxes and refuels you. It gets you ready for a new day or a fresh start. It's the practices, rituals, and meaningful activities that you do, just for you, that help you feel safe, grounded, happy, and fulfilled.

The activities that qualify as self-care are amazingly unique and personalized to who you are, what you like, and, in large part, what your astrological sign is. If you're asking questions about what self-care practices are best for those ruled by water and born under the nurturing eye of Cancer, you'll find answers—and restoration—in Part 2. But, no matter which of those self-care activities speak to you and your unique place in the universe on any given day, it will fall into one of the following self-care categories—each of which pertains to a different aspect of your life:

* Physical self-care
* Emotional self-care
* Social self-care
* Mental self-care
* Spiritual self-care
* Practical self-care

When you practice all of these unique types of self-care—and prioritize your practice to ensure you are choosing the best options for your unique sign and governing element—know that you are actively working to create the version of yourself that the universe intends you to be.

Physical Self-Care

When you practice physical self-care, you make the decision to look after and restore the one physical body that has been bestowed upon you. Care for it. Use it in the best way you can imagine, for that is what the universe wishes you to do. You can't light the world on fire or move mountains if you're not doing everything you can to take care of your physical health.

Emotional Self-Care

Emotional self-care is when you take the time to acknowledge and care for your inner self, your emotional well-being. Whether you're angry or frustrated, happy or joyful, or somewhere in between, emotional self-care happens when you choose to sit with your emotions: when you step away from the noise of daily life that often drowns out or tamps down your authentic self. Emotional self-care lets you see your inner you as the cosmos intend. Once you identify your true emotions, you can either accept them and continue to move forward on your journey or you can try to change any negative emotions for the better. The more you acknowledge your feelings and practice emotional self-care, the more you'll feel the positivity that the universe and your life holds for you.

Social Self-Care

You practice social self-care when you nurture your relationships with others, be they friends, coworkers, or family members. In today's hectic world it's easy to let relationships fall to the wayside, but it's so important to share your life with others—and let others share their lives with you. Social self-care is reciprocal and often karmic. The support and love that you put out into the universe through social self-care is given back to you by those you socialize with—often tenfold.

Mental Self-Care

Mental self-care is anything that keeps your mind working quickly and critically. It helps you cut through the fog of the day, week, or year and ensures that your quick wit and sharp mind are intact and working the way the cosmos intended. Making sure your mind is fit helps you problem-solve, decreases stress since you're not feeling overwhelmed, and keeps you feeling on top of your mental game—no matter your sign or your situation.

Spiritual Self-Care

Spiritual self-care is self-care that allows you to tap into your soul and the soul of the universe and uncover its secrets. Rather than focusing on a particular religion or set of religious beliefs, these types of self-care activities reconnect you with a higher power: the sense that something out there is bigger than you. When you meditate, you connect. When you pray, you connect. Whenever you do something that allows you to experience and marry yourself to the vastness that is the cosmos, you practice spiritual self-care.

Practical Self-Care

Self-care is what you do to take care of yourself, and practical self-care, while not as expansive as the other types, is made up of the seemingly small day-to-day tasks that bring you peace and accomplishment. These practical self-care rituals are important, but are often overlooked. Scheduling a doctor's appointment that you've been putting off is practical self-care. Getting your hair cut is practical self-care. Anything you can check off your list of things to be accomplished gives you a sacred space to breathe and allows the universe more room to bring a beautiful sense of cosmic fulfillment your way.

What Self-Care Isn't

Self-care is restorative. Self-care is clarifying. Self-care is whatever you need to do to make yourself feel secure in the universe.

Now that you know what self-care is, it's also important that you're able to see what self-care isn't. Self-care is not something that you force yourself to do because you think it will be good for you. Some signs are energy in motion and sitting still goes against their place in the universe. Those signs won't feel refreshed by lying in a hammock or sitting down to meditate. Other signs aren't able to ground themselves unless they've found a self-care practice that protects their cosmic need for peace and quiet. Those signs won't find parties, concerts, and loud venues soothing or satisfying. If a certain ritual doesn't bring you peace, clarity, or satisfaction, then it's not right for your sign and you should find something that speaks to you more clearly.

There's a difference though between not finding satisfaction in a ritual that you've tried and not wanting to try a self-care activity because you're tired or stuck in a comfort zone. Sometimes going to the gym or meeting up with friends is the self-care practice that you need to experience—whether engaging in it feels like a downer or not. So consider how you feel when you're actually doing the activity. If it feels invigorating to get on the treadmill or you feel delight when you actually catch up with your friend, the ritual is doing what it should be doing and clearing space for you—among other benefits...

The Benefits of Self-Care

The benefits of self-care are boundless and there's none that's superior to helping you put rituals in place to feel more at home in your body, in your spirit, and in your unique home in the cosmos. There are, however, other benefits to engaging in the practice of self-care that you should know.

Rejuvenates Your Immune System

No matter which rituals are designated for you by the stars, your sign, and its governing element, self-care helps both your body and mind rest, relax, and recuperate. The practice of self-care activates the parasympathetic nervous system (often called the rest and digest system), which slows your heart rate, calms the body, and overall helps your body relax and release tension. This act of decompression gives your body the space it needs to build up and strengthen your immune system, which protects you from illness.

Helps You Reconnect—with Yourself

When you practice the ritual of self-care—especially when you customize this practice based on your personal sign and governing element—you learn what you like to do and what you need to do to replenish yourself. Knowing yourself better, and allowing yourself the time and space that you need to focus on your personal needs and desires, gives you the gifts of self-confidence and self-knowledge. Setting time aside to focus on your needs also helps you put busy, must-do things aside, which gives you time to reconnect with yourself and who you are deep inside.

Increases Compassion

Perhaps one of the most important benefits of creating a self-care ritual is that, by focusing on yourself, you become more compassionate to others as well. When you truly take the time to care for yourself and make yourself and your importance in the universe a priority in your own life, you're then able to care for others and see their needs and desires in a new way. You can't pour from an empty dipper, and self-care allows you the space and clarity to do what you can to send compassion out into the world.

Starting a Self-Care Routine

Self-care should be treated as a ritual in your life, something you make the time to pause for, no matter what. You are important. You deserve rejuvenation and a sense of relaxation. You need to open your soul to the gifts that the universe is giving you, and self-care provides you with a way to ensure you're ready to receive those gifts. To begin a self-care routine, start by making yourself the priority. Do the customized rituals in Part 2 with intention, knowing the universe has already given them to you, by virtue of your sign and your governing element.

Now that you understand the role that self-care will hold in your life, let's take a closer look at the connection between self-care and astrology.

CHAPTER 2

SELF-CARE AND ASTROLOGY

Astrology is the study of the connection between the objects in the heavens (the planets, the stars) and what happens here on earth. Just as the movements of the planets and other heavenly bodies influence the ebb and flow of the tides, so do they influence you—your body, your mind, your spirit. This relationship is ever present and is never more important—or personal—than when viewed through the lens of self-care.

In this chapter you'll learn how the locations of these celestial bodies at the time of your birth affect you and define the self-care activities that will speak directly to you as a Leo, an Aries, a Capricorn, or any of the other zodiac signs. You'll see how the zodiac influences every part of your being and why ignoring its lessons can leave you feeling frustrated and unfulfilled. You'll also realize that, when you perform the rituals of self-care based on your sign, the wisdom of the cosmos will lead you down a path of fulfillment and restoration—to the return of who you really are, deep inside.

Zodiac Polarities

In astrology, all signs are mirrored by other signs that are on the opposite side of the zodiac. This polarity ensures that the zodiac is balanced and continues to flow with an unbreakable, even stream of energy. There are two different polarities in the zodiac and each is called by a number of different names:

* Yang/masculine/positive polarity
* Yin/feminine/negative polarity

Each polar opposite embodies a number of opposing traits, qualities, and attributes that will influence which self-care practices will work for or against your sign and your own personal sense of cosmic balance.

Yang

Whether male or female, those who fall under yang, or masculine, signs are extroverted and radiate their energy outward. They are spontaneous, active, bold, and fearless. They move forward in life with the desire to enjoy everything the world has to offer to them, and they work hard to transfer their inspiration and positivity to others so that those individuals may experience the same gifts that the universe offers them. All signs governed by the fire and air elements are yang and hold the potential for these dominant qualities. We will refer to them with masculine pronouns. These signs are:

* Aries
* Leo
* Sagittarius
* Gemini
* Libra
* Aquarius

There are people who hold yang energy who are introverted and retiring. However, by practicing self-care that is customized for your sign and understanding the potential ways to use your energy, you can find a way—perhaps one that's unique to you—to claim your native buoyancy and dominance and engage with the path that the universe opens for you.

Yin

Whether male or female, those who fall under yin, or feminine, signs are introverted and radiate inwardly. They draw people and experiences to them rather than seeking people and experiences in an extroverted way. They move forward in life with an energy that is reflective, receptive, and focused on communication and achieving shared goals. All signs governed by the earth and water elements are yin and hold the potential for these reflective qualities. We will refer to them with feminine pronouns. These signs are:

* Taurus
* Virgo
* Capricorn
* Cancer
* Scorpio
* Pisces

As there are people with yang energy who are introverted and retiring, there are also people with yin energy who are outgoing and extroverted. And by practicing self-care rituals that speak to your particular sign, energy, and governing body, you will reveal your true self and the balance of energy will be maintained.

Governing Elements

Each astrological sign has a governing element that defines their energy orientation and influences both the way the sign moves through the universe and relates to self-care. The elements are fire, earth, air, and water. All the signs in each element share certain characteristics, along with having their own sign-specific qualities:

* **Fire:** Fire signs are adventurous, bold, and energetic. They enjoy the heat and warm environments and look to the sun and fire as a means to recharge their depleted batteries. They're competitive, outgoing, and passionate. The fire signs are Aries, Leo, and Sagittarius.
* **Earth:** Earth signs all share a common love and tendency toward a practical, material, sensual, and economic orientation. The earth signs are Taurus, Virgo, and Capricorn.
* **Air:** Air is the most ephemeral element and those born under this element are thinkers, innovators, and communicators. The air signs are Gemini, Libra, and Aquarius.
* **Water:** Water signs are instinctual, compassionate, sensitive, and emotional. The water signs are Cancer, Scorpio, and Pisces.

Chapter 3 teaches you all about the ways your specific governing element influences and drives your connection to your cosmically harmonious self-care rituals, but it's important that you realize how important these elemental traits are to your self-care practice and to the activities that will help restore and reveal your true self.

Sign Qualities

Each of the astrological elements governs three signs. Each of these three signs is also given its own quality or mode, which corresponds to a different part of each season: the beginning, the middle, or the end.

* **Cardinal signs:** The cardinal signs initiate and lead in each season. Like something that is just starting out, they are actionable, enterprising, and assertive, and are born leaders. The cardinal signs are Aries, Cancer, Libra, and Capricorn.
* **Fixed signs:** The fixed signs come into play when the season is well established. They are definite, consistent, reliable, motivated by principles, and powerfully stubborn. The fixed signs are Taurus, Leo, Scorpio, and Aquarius.
* **Mutable signs:** The mutable signs come to the forefront when the seasons are changing. They are part of one season, but also part of the next. They are adaptable, versatile, and flexible. The mutable signs are Gemini, Virgo, Sagittarius, and Pisces.

Each of these qualities tells you a lot about yourself and who you are. They also give you invaluable information about the types of self-care rituals that your sign will find the most intuitive and helpful.

Ruling Planets

In addition to qualities and elements, each specific sign is ruled by a particular planet that lends its personality to those born under that sign. Again, these sign-specific traits give you valuable insight into the personality of the signs and the self-care rituals that may best rejuvenate them. The signs that correspond to each planet—and the ways that those planetary influences determine your self-care options—are as follows:

* **Aries:** Ruled by Mars, Aries is passionate, energetic, and determined.
* **Taurus:** Ruled by Venus, Taurus is sensual, romantic, and fertile.
* **Gemini:** Ruled by Mercury, Gemini is intellectual, changeable, and talkative.
* **Cancer:** Ruled by the Moon, Cancer is nostalgic, emotional, and home loving.
* **Leo:** Ruled by the Sun, Leo is fiery, dramatic, and confident.
* **Virgo:** Ruled by Mercury, Virgo is intellectual, analytical, and responsive.
* **Libra:** Ruled by Venus, Libra is beautiful, romantic, and graceful.
* **Scorpio:** Ruled by Mars and Pluto, Scorpio is intense, powerful, and magnetic.
* **Sagittarius:** Ruled by Jupiter, Sagittarius is optimistic, boundless, and larger than life.

* **Capricorn:** Ruled by Saturn, Capricorn is wise, patient, and disciplined.
* **Aquarius:** Ruled by Uranus, Aquarius is independent, unique, and eccentric.
* **Pisces:** Ruled by Neptune and Jupiter, Pisces is dreamy, sympathetic, and idealistic.

A Word on Sun Signs

When someone is a Leo, Aries, Sagittarius, or any of the other zodiac signs, it means that the sun was positioned in this constellation in the heavens when they were born. Your Sun sign is a dominant factor in defining your personality, your best self-care practices, and your soul nature. Every person also has the position of the Moon, Mercury, Venus, Mars, Jupiter, Saturn, Uranus, Neptune, and Pluto. These planets can be in any of the elements: fire signs, earth signs, air signs, or water signs. If you have your entire chart calculated by an astrologer or on an Internet site, you can see the whole picture and learn about all your elements. Someone born under Leo with many signs in another element will not be as concentrated in the fire element as someone with five or six planets in Leo. Someone born in Pisces with many signs in another element will not be as concentrated in the water element as someone with five or six planets in Pisces. And so on. Astrology is a complex system and has many shades of meaning. For our purposes looking at the self-care practices designated by your Sun sign, or what most people consider *their* sign, will give you the information you need to move forward and find fulfillment and restoration.

CHAPTER 3

ESSENTIAL ELEMENTS: WATER

Water is the fourth and final element of creation. It is essential for the planet and for our physical existence. It is amorphous, meaning it assumes the shape of its container or geographical location and solidifies only when frozen. Those who have water as their governing element—Cancer, Scorpio, and Pisces—all have a special energy signature and connection with water that guides all aspects of their lives. Water signs are intuitive and tend to live on waves of feeling. They are reflective, responsive, and fertile, and are often more sensitive than other signs. Their path in life is to quell their overwhelming emotions and use their instincts for love and compassion toward themselves and others.

Their approach to self-care must include these goals. Let's take a look at the mythological importance of water and its fluid counterparts, the basic characteristics of the three water signs, and what they all have in common when it comes to self-care.

The Mythology of Water

In Greek mythology water is linked to the god of the sea, Poseidon. Poseidon was brother to Zeus and Hades, and one of the six children conceived by Rhea and Cronos. His father, Cronos, ruled the universe, but was eventually overthrown by Zeus. After their father's collapse of power, Zeus, Hades, and Poseidon decided to divide the earth between the three of them. Poseidon became the lord of the sea, while Zeus became lord of Mount Olympus and sky, and Hades became the lord of the underworld.

The sea god was especially important in the ancient world as sea travel and navigation formed the principal trade and travel routes. Throughout mythology, going to sea was seen as a precarious adventure, and sailors often prayed to Poseidon for safe return and calm waters. Many myths feature Poseidon saving a ship at the last moment. In other myths he is not so merciful.

Like Poseidon, water signs make their decisions based off emotion. Their gut feelings guide them. This makes water signs highly compassionate and understanding, but it can also make them moody at times. Water signs may try to keep their emotions balanced in the hope of staying in control of their feelings, rather than allowing their feelings to control them. This desire drives their likes and dislikes, personality traits, and approaches to self-care.

The Element of Water

In terms of astrology, the water signs are called the feeling signs. They feel first, and think and speak later. They are very familiar with the emotional expression of tears, laughter, anger, joy, and grief. They often wear their heart on their sleeve and are extremely sentimental. Scorpio is somewhat of an exception to this characterization, but, nevertheless, she has a sensitive feeling mechanism. A water sign's energy moves inward, and they draw people and experiences to them rather than overtly seeking out people and experiences. For example, Scorpio's bravery means she is always open to new adventures. Cancer's loyalty encourages her to stick close to family and friends. And Pisces's creative intuition makes her a wonderful problem-solver when faced with a difficult conundrum.

Astrological Symbols

The astrological symbols (also called the zodiacal symbols) of the water signs also give you hints as to how the water signs move through the world. The symbols of all the water signs are creatures connected with the sea, the cradle of life:

* Scorpio is the Scorpion (and the Eagle and the Phoenix)
* Cancer is the Crab
* Pisces is the two Fish tied together

Scorpio has a complex set of symbols because there are varieties of scorpions, both in the sea and on land, but the sea is home to all these sensitive water signs. Scorpio uses her stinger to sting first rather than take the time to ask questions. Cancer the Crab holds on to her home tenaciously and never approaches anything directly. Instead, she moves from side to side to go forward in zigzag motions. And Pisces's two Fish tied together symbolize duality—one of the fish staying above the water, paying attention to the earth, and the other living in the sea, where dreams and the imagination rule.

Signs and Seasonal Modes

Each of the elements in astrology also has a sign that corresponds to a different part of each season.

* **Cardinal:** Cancer, as the first water sign, comes at the summer solstice, when summer begins. She is a cardinal sign and the leader of the water signs. She may lead indirectly, but has a powerful desire to be in control.
* **Fixed:** Scorpio, the next water sign, is a fixed water sign, and she rules when autumn is well established. The fixed signs are definite, motivated by principles, and powerfully stubborn.
* **Mutable:** And Pisces, the last water sign and the last sign of the zodiac, is a mutable sign. She moves us from winter to the spring equinox in Aries. The major characteristic of mutable, or changeable, signs is flexibility.

If you know your element and whether you are a cardinal, fixed, or mutable sign, you know a lot about yourself. This is invaluable for self-care and is reflected in the customized water sign self-care rituals found in Part 2.

Water Signs and Self-Care

Self-care comes naturally to water signs. Oftentimes, they find it is essential to take care of themselves because they feel acutely when something is askew inside them. They may complain bitterly about not feeling well, or about their sensitivities or the weather, but they generally know what to do to get back on course. Physical self-care is the hardest area for the water signs to master, because they do not like to do things unless they feel like doing them. Once they have a routine that has proven will make them feel better, they will stick to it, but before they adopt that routine, they are often hit-or-miss when it comes to diet, exercise, and medical checkups. Water signs are also very in tune with alternative cures and what their ancestors did for self-care.

Another essential factor in water sign self-care is the atmosphere of the gym or exercise location. Generally, water signs do not like crowds. If it is 5 p.m. and people are pounding out their aggressions from work on the treadmill, most water signs will choose to wait for the crowds to thin, or go earlier in the day. However, one of the great encouragements for water signs is the use of a shower or pool—a water source that they can include in their routine is a great enticement for water signs. Water signs may choose to attend classes at the gym, but most of the time they prefer to make sure that they are not overly influenced by other people's vibes.

Water signs are especially drawn to natural surroundings when it comes to self-care. Walking by a pond or lake is perhaps the best exercise for them, as it combines physical, mental, and spiritual practice. In a low-pressure environment, water signs feel that all their activities are worthwhile, both in terms of money and time. They are very aware of the money they spend and tend to be prudent and almost stingy with funds. And there is a direct relationship between their feeling of well-being and how much money they have in the bank.

Water signs are nurturers and make it a priority to take care of family and friends. It is always best for water signs to frame their self-care in terms of their familial feelings about something. For example, the statement "If you quit eating all this junk, you will help your family by setting a good example and you will feel better" is a winning one for water signs, marrying their love for their family with their own self-care. Once the water sign gets the feeling that they can extend the love and care of their family to themselves through self-care, they feel more comfortable designating attention to wellness practices.

In terms of emotional self-care, the most important factor for water signs is to avoid exaggerating their reactions to events or people. The more water signs can stay in the here and now, the less they will feel there are imaginary scenarios of people working against them. They are so sensitive that it is very easy for them to lapse into being self-conscious. A very good technique for water signs is to play a game asking themselves the question, "How would I feel if I were that person?" This thinking pattern encourages compassion rather than self-centeredness in water signs.

Water signs have a gift for feeling. In today's society we tend to diminish the importance of being emotional. Water signs may feel they have to do all the heavy lifting in the emotional department, which may make them feel lonely. Water signs are naturally empathetic, so the trick for them is to balance how they feel about other people and extend those good feelings to themselves. Feelings are different from intellectual, inspirational, and practical concerns. The water signs symbolize the potential of members of the human family to share their individual feelings.

So, now that you know what water signs need to practice self-care, let's look at each of the characteristics of Cancer and how she can maintain her gifts.

CHAPTER 4

SELF-CARE FOR CANCER

✳

Dates: June 21–July 22
Element: Water
Polarity: Yin
Quality: Cardinal
Symbol: Crab
Ruler: The Moon

Cancer is the first water sign of the zodiac. She is yin and a cardinal sign, reigning in the summer solstice, when the sun is at its height and daylight abounds. But the light that influences Cancer the most is the reflected light of the moon at night. Holding these polarities (day and night) together are the many feelings and moods that Cancer passes through each day. She is hard to pin down, as she is always feeling out a situation before making any decisions—with no rules, just a sense.

The sign of Cancer is sometimes not easy for male Cancerians. It contradicts the stereotypical ideal of masculinity, as Cancer is sensitive and desires emotional expression. One way a Cancer man may successfully balance his Cancerian nature and traditional masculinity is by channeling his feelings into his home life rather than pushing them aside.

Cancerian moodiness may suggest a shy and retiring personality; however, Cancer is a leadership sign. She leads indirectly, through encouragement and support, rather than through direct instruction and authority. Cancer's handwringing, tears, anxiety, and back-and-forth feelings can try the patience of everyone around her. Others may be convinced that Cancer will never accomplish what she sets out to do, but time proves that she achieves her goals at her own pace.

The Crab, Cancer's symbol, is a half-land and half-water creature. Symbolically, Cancer will make a move on dry land (logic and physical life), and then dip back into the water (feelings and spiritual life) to renew herself. The water allows her to tap into her intuition in order to feel out whether it is safe to proceed.

The Crab symbol comes from a Greek myth. In the myth Cancer, originally known as Karkinos, was a giant crab who was ordered by the goddess Hera to bite the hero Herakles (popularly known as Hercules) on the foot during battle. Karkinos disabled Herakles for a time, but Herakles subsequently crushed Karkinos. For his valor, Hera rewarded the crab by placing him in the constellation now known as Cancer. Cancer should take this myth to heart as a reminder of her courage.

The other ancient foundation for Cancer is the Great Mother. In astrology the Moon represents women and all motherly instincts. Ruled by the Moon, Cancer has a natural affinity for babies and anyone who needs to be taken care of. A Cancerian parent fiercely protects her kids. She is wary of anything that could harm her family in any way.

Self-Care and Cancer

In terms of self-care, the two primary motivations for Cancer are family and the lunar cycle. Cancer works hard to see her family grow and prosper. She accumulates money to make this happen, and watches her saving and spending carefully. If a self-care program can prove to Cancer that it will save money in the long run, she will be motivated to stick with it.

Cancer is also driven by the desire to set a healthy example for her children and other family members. If Cancer does not have any kids or close family members, she will develop strong familial bonds with people and groups she encounters. This is a key for her success in exercise and diet plans. She wants to feel affection for a group effort, and feel cheered on by the instructor's and members' approval. Many gym and diet programs foster a camaraderie that creates a family feeling, and this dynamic will encourage watery Cancer to achieve her goals.

The lunar cycle is important to keep in mind with Cancerian wellness, as it can have a direct effect on her mood, thus steering her motivation toward or away from a self-care activity. To keep up with any self-care program, watery Cancer should understand that even if she doesn't feel like doing something one day, she may feel like doing it the next. She should avoid making hard-and-fast decisions, because moods will change.

Every month there is a new moon and a full moon. Cancer will feel energized and inspired during the new moon. She should begin all new projects during this time, from work to self-care. The full moon, which takes place about two weeks after the new moon, represents the culmination of energy. Cancer may feel the need to howl a little during this phase.

After the full moon begins the waning lunar phase. This is when Cancer should ground her plans for self-care, relationships, and anything else, by reviewing the feelings that began during the new moon. Last comes the period of the lunar cycle traditionally called the dark of the moon because Luna, the Roman goddess of the moon, is not visible. This is a time of rest for Cancer. She may sleep more and have very illuminating dreams. This lunar cycle affects all signs but is strongest with Cancer because the Moon is her planetary ruler.

Cancer Rules the Breasts and Stomach

Cancer rules the breasts and stomach, so self-care related to these areas is especially important. For women, breasts can be a source of nourishment and a symbol of sexuality. For men, strong pectoral muscles may be a hard-won goal. Cancerian self-care for both men and women is very simple: get regular checkups. The Cancer woman should also take extra care in breast health through performing self-checks at least once a month. These checks can be done in the shower and are a good way to get to know what is normal for her breasts and to check for any changes.

The stomach is a more complicated part of the body, as it is linked directly to Cancer's many changing emotions. Depending on the situation, Cancer may have butterflies in her stomach or feel unable to eat anything. Apart from enhancing emotions, the stomach can also tell Cancer whether or not something is right. The saying *trust your gut* is advice Cancer should follow. If she pays attention to how her stomach reacts to a person, project, or environment, she can automatically know whether it is right for her.

If Cancer is not feeling well, she should have a doctor check her digestive system, as it holds the answers to many health problems. Asking her doctor (who is familiar with her health and medications) about using a probiotic or digestive enzymes is an excellent self-care practice for Cancer. If all is well with the stomach, Cancer will be balanced and content.

Eating in crowded, bustling restaurants is not conducive to a happy meal for Cancer. To enjoy and fully digest her meal, she needs to feel that things around her are calm. She also loves sitting in booths, rather than at tables, where she will be in closer proximity to other people. Although there are some very well-known Cancerian chefs, Cancer typically prefers uncomplicated food. She also delights in dishes that remind her of fond memories. Fusion foods with elaborate garnishes won't appeal.

Cancer also enjoys feeding the stomachs of friends and family members. Cooking for a gathering or family dinner and providing nourishment for others is an essential part of Cancer self-care.

Cancer and Self-Care Success

A pitfall to success in Cancer self-care is her slow-moving energy. The water always appeals to Cancer, but, oftentimes, she does not like to swim. She may be afraid of the water in these instances, or may just not be interested. However, if she incorporates the lunar cycle into her schedule, she will have a better chance of sticking to a self-care routine even on days when she may not feel like it.

Exercise with music, such as ballroom dancing or rocking out solo at home, provides enough movement for Cancer while appealing to her need for self-expression. As a water sign, she will also enjoy a walk by a pond, river, or ocean. No matter what mood she is in, these exercises will provide a release that also keeps her active.

Another pitfall for Cancer's self-care program is her over-indulgence in sentiment that impedes action. As an emotional sign, she can spend more time fretting over what she has done, or might do, rather than taking action. Learning to negotiate this tendency is an important life skill that Cancer will continually work at.

Perhaps the most important pathway for Cancer's self-care success, however, is through her incredible connection to the subconscious. And her feeling memory extends far beyond her own past—into the sentiments of different time periods. She is acutely aware of mass consciousness and trends in the wider society. Her quest is to learn from the past and share her unique perspective with the world. So let's take a look at some self-care activities especially designed for you, Cancer.

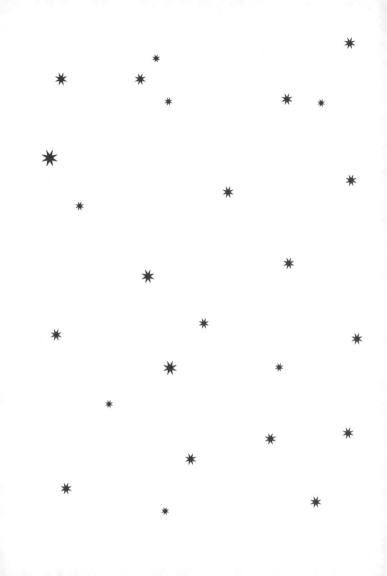

♋

PART 2

SELF-CARE
RITUALS
—— FOR ——
CANCER

Get Motivated

If you find that you are feeling unmotivated to work out, start by listening to your favorite music to get amped up. Sometimes just feeling the beat can jump-start your energy level and get your blood flowing. If you are working out at home, you may even want to try dancing around as your entire workout. Dancing for 30 minutes is great cardio. Just blast your favorite tunes and let your body move naturally. Mix up the playlist tempo to keep things interesting. No slow songs allowed!

Ease Your Worries with Bergamot

Sensitive Cancer's thoughts can be hard to slow down. With so many emotions moving through her each day, she can easily fall into a cycle of overthinking. Bergamot essential oil can help! This citrus scent is perfect for Cancer, as it soothes the nerves and reduces stress—just be sure to use a small amount, as it can become a bit more powerful than watery Cancer prefers.

Bergamot may also promote stomach health. It is claimed that the oil both activates and increases the release of digestive acids and enzymes, facilitating digestion. As Cancer rules the stomach, healthy digestion is crucial to her overall wellness.

Take deep breaths as you massage a drop or two of the oil (diluted according to instructions—also be aware that topical use of bergamot can increase your sensitivity to sunlight) into your temples or stomach area, or diffuse it in your bedroom or other comfortable living space where you can stretch out and relax.

Strike a Half-Moon Pose

Celebrate your Moon mother with the perfect Cancerian pose! This yoga position promotes balance between Cancer's light (summer season) and dark (ruling planet) halves. This is not a beginners' pose, so make sure to practice this with your yoga instructor for technique guidance.

Yoga teachers have tips on performing this tricky pose, including using various transition poses (such as Triangle Pose), blocks, or even the support of the wall. Work with them to find the perfect Half-Moon Pose method for you!

Make Water a Part of Your Life

You may think that all water signs are naturally drawn to water in every capacity, but this isn't necessarily true. Every water sign is different and has different preferences. While most water signs take comfort in water-based activities, such as swimming, diving, and water aerobics, others prefer to simply be near water, but not in it. Wherever you fall on this spectrum, water is an important grounding mechanism for you. It calms you, makes you feel safe, and helps orient you when you are feeling lost. Make water a part of your life in whatever way you feel most comfortable.

Affirm Your Abilities

With Cancer's care for others, her own needs can fall to the wayside. She freely gives, asking for nothing in return; thus, people forget that though she does not ask, Cancer also needs a little encouragement. When you feel self-doubt creeping in, you can give yourself that much-needed confidence boost through the use of an affirmation. An affirmation, written down and revisited as needed, will serve as a reminder of your abilities.

The perfect affirmation for Cancer is "I build a lighted house and therein dwell." There is a reason people come to you in their time of need. Just as a lighthouse is the illuminating siren for ships caught in a storm, you are a beacon of knowledge and insight. It's no wonder people trust your thoughts—now it's time for *you* to trust them.

Choose Flowing Exercises

As a water sign, you are drawn to fluid movements. When it comes to exercise, look for things that give your body freedom to move in the way it wants to. The last thing you want is to be restrained. Try tai chi or an aerobic dance class. Even Pilates can be soothing for water signs, as it helps build muscle and keeps you moving in a natural way.

Promote Emotional Balance with Pearls

J ust like watery Cancer, the pearl has a special connection to the ocean—in fact, it was born from it. The
pearl is also linked to Cancer's ruler, the Moon. This
captivating milky white treasure doesn't just resemble
the moon—it also balances your body's hormones with
it. In matching your emotions with the moon's lunar
cycles, the pearl helps to ease negative feelings while
encouraging love, as well as an appreciation for the
here and now. Wear pearls on a bracelet, cufflinks, or
a necklace, where they will be at your fingertips. They
will ensure that your feet are always firmly planted on
the ground.

Stick to a Routine

Routine can be boring for a water sign, but it is key to a solid self-care regimen. It may take discipline to stick to a routine, but without a well-constructed plan, apathy will take over and you'll find yourself doing nothing to improve your overall wellness. Make sure you vary your activities to keep things fresh and new. It may help to buy a large desk calendar and mark off when you are doing what activity. This will help keep you on track and will take any indecisiveness off the table.

Meteorate On Your Mantra

Insightful Cancer is deeply connected to the sub-conscious. So many thoughts and emotions are constantly coursing through you—and not just your own, but everyone else's as well. Fortunately, you can quiet all of this mental noise and refocus your energy by reciting a special mantra.

A mantra is a unique phrase that you repeat out loud in order to center yourself and tune out unhelpful thoughts. A great mantra for Cancer is "The past is rich, but the here and now is better." Use this mantra to ground yourself in the present when you feel your mind becoming tangled in outside stress and past events—especially when those thoughts and memories will only lead to worry and self-doubt.

Stretch

———————

The type of exercise you do as a water sign is very important. Many water signs have smooth muscles that do not usually bulk up, so doing exercises that are designed to add heft to your muscle won't be particularly beneficial. Instead, you should look for exercises that stretch your muscles, such as yoga. You don't even have to go to a yoga class to try it out. There are plenty of online videos for beginner yogis to try—just stick to the basics.

If yoga isn't your favorite, you can still make stretching an essential part of your wellness routine by stretching before and after every workout. It may even help to do some gentle stretches before bed to keep your muscles limber and flexible.

Sip a Blue Moon Cocktail

───────────

What better drink for Moon-ruled Cancer than the blue moon cocktail? This striking purple libation invokes the deep, reflective vibes of the moon wrapped in a dark night. Romantic Cancer will also love the history of this cocktail, which was created in the 1940s to embody the passion of New York City in that era, when flashy dresses and an appreciation for abstract expressionist art took hold.

To mix up a blue moon, simply add 2 ounces dry gin, ½ ounce Crème Yvette, and ½ ounce fresh lemon juice to a shaker filled with ice. Shake, and then strain into a chilled cocktail glass and garnish with a lemon twist.

Watch Your Salt (and Water)

—————

You've probably heard that our bodies are made up of more than 50 percent water. Water signs tend to hold on to water more than other signs do, which means they often have a softness to their faces and bodies. It may seem counterproductive, but drinking the right amount of water daily may, in certain circumstances, help reduce water retention, as well as flush toxins. Sometimes our bodies retain water in response to dehydration. Try to meet the recommended guidelines for how much water you should drink every day (depending on sex, lifestyle, climate, and health).

You can also watch how much salt you consume. Too much sodium (either in table salt or processed foods and soft drinks) increases your risk of water retention. If you do experience water retention symptoms, visit your doctor for advice.

Magnetize Abundance
with Lucky Bamboo

The lucky bamboo plant is renowned as a good luck charm that symbolizes prosperity. Intuitive Cancer understands the importance of saving wisely.

This plant is also a key element in feng shui, which uses nature to maximize a person's positive energy, or chi. When the full moon has your emotions running high, a lucky bamboo plant placed near the front entrance of your home will help you restore inner balance and displace negativity.

Turn to Nature

Stress happens to everyone; it's how you handle it that makes a difference. For water signs the best way to beat stress is to retreat to a safe space: nature. If you have the opportunity to spend time by a body of water, like a creek, river, or, ideally, the beach, do so as often as possible. Just listen to the sound the water makes as it moves, lapping against rocks or sand, and let the stress melt away from your muscles. If you don't have easy access to a body of water, download and listen to some water sounds outside. It's not quite the same, but it will mimic the calming experience of being by the water.

Create an Empowering Playlist

Cancer, as an emotional sign, is highly sensitive to her surroundings, including sounds. The right tune can uplift her mood and leave her energized, while the wrong one can lead to feelings of melancholy or irritation. So what songs will Cancer enjoy?

Music that blends energy with emotion is perfect for lifting Cancer's spirits when she may be feeling down or uninspired. Fellow Cancerians know better than anyone how to amplify your unique celestial energy, so be sure to include them in your playlist. The talents of Cyndi Lauper, Huey Lewis, Carly Simon, and Carlos Santana are guaranteed to get you moving to the rhythm.

Laugh As Much As Possible

———————

Laughter can soothe the soul, especially the soul of a weary water sign. You tend to feel deeply, and need a healthy release to let go of those heavy emotions. Laughter can be that release. If you don't laugh, you may start to get bogged down with too many negative feelings. The only way to survive in life is to see the comedy in things. Water signs are especially good at this, but, sometimes, they need a little push. When you are feeling down, go to a funny movie or seek out a stand-up comedian putting on a show.

Make Your Own Holiday Cards

Cancer is a sentimental sign, which is why holidays are her favorite times of the year. What better way to spread your love this season than with home-made cards? Yes, a commercial card is easy to add to your shopping list, but a card that you have created on your own expresses your feelings more than any mass-marketed poem ever could. You can also tailor your cards to each person, depending on the colors or objects they like. If you have a talent for drawing, this is the perfect way to showcase it. Although your loved ones will appreciate the effort and humor of a stick figure too!

Avoid Crowds

You are a sensitive soul, water sign, one who tends to absorb the vibrations and energy coming from other people. Because of this, it's best for you to avoid large crowds, especially if you are feeling vulnerable or sad. Being in a large group of strangers will just exacerbate those negative feelings you are struggling with, and may even make you feel more alone than you already do. Instead, stay home and allow yourself some quality relaxation time. Give yourself permission to lounge around and be lazy. Enjoy your own company!

Get Lost in a Book

―――――――――――

A good book not only provides the perfect escape from everyday life, but it also allows you to expand your knowledge, and view a topic from different perspectives. As a nurturing sign, Cancer often gives all of her time and energy away to others, leaving her exhausted and overwhelmed. Reading is a great way to recharge your batteries and enjoy some much-needed alone time. But what does Cancer enjoy reading?

You love books that make you reflect on your own experiences, as well as the unique experiences of others. It is through this kind of deep, introspective thought that you draw wisdom. A work by a kindred Cancerian spirit, such as Ernest Hemingway, Octavia E. Butler, Markus Zusak, or Dan Brown, may also top your reading list.

Wash It Off

As a water sign, you are used to being affected by other people's energy and the energy of the atmosphere around you. It is essential for your emotional health that you wash away any feelings you may have absorbed from others throughout the day. Make a point to take a shower or bath every night to cleanse your emotional aura. You may even find dry brushing before you bathe to be beneficial. Not only does dry brushing help loosen and remove dead skin from your body, it can be a wonderfully cathartic experience for water signs, especially if you envision the ritual as also sloughing away any emotional burdens you have picked up over the past few hours.

Snack on Cucumber and Watercress Sandwiches

Perfect little triangles with simple, refreshing colors, cucumber and watercress sandwiches are an ideal treat for Cancer. Prone to indulging in not-so-healthy foods, Cancer will love how light, nutritious, and yet scrumptious these sandwiches are. Additionally, they are sliced small, so she can enjoy more than one! Cucumber and watercress are also Cancer-ruled, as they contain quite a bit of her watery element. Bring these sandwiches to your next party with friends or family, or prepare them for a sophisticated touch to a quiet afternoon at home.

Keep It Simple

When it comes to fashion, water signs like to keep things simple and classic. Their favorite colors for clothing are muted tones, like navy blue, black, gray, and white, along with pops of color, like turquoise. Once a water sign finds a style that they are comfortable with, they'll stick to it. Changing their style requires a lot of energy, so it's easier for them to stay with what works.

Don't be surprised if it takes you a little while to get acclimated to a new fashion accessory or style of dressing. If you get the urge, though, do try out something new. You can always go back to your favorite staple items if you are uncomfortable.

Set Good Bathroom Vibes

Make your bathroom into the oasis you deserve! Having the perfect vessel to indulge your watery tendencies is essential for a water sign's self-care. Invest in a deep tub for your bathroom that you can soak in when you are feeling stressed—the deeper and roomier the better. Buy luxurious bubble baths and bath bombs to use when you draw a bath. Additionally, make sure that you have good water pressure for your shower. Lastly, choose bathroom tile that reflects water themes and colors, such as light blue, white, and green.

Enjoy a Meal at a Diner

Sentimental Cancer enjoys anything that offers a homey feel and delicious comfort food. With down-home meals at a reasonable price, and large booths to seat all of your friends or family members, a classic diner is the perfect choice for your next dinner out. The retro décor and crooning jukebox will have you feeling blissfully nostalgic (even if it's for a decade that was before your time). Invite someone from an older generation to come along and share their stories from the "good ol' days."

Sail Off to Sleep

Fortunately, water signs tend to fall asleep relatively easily, but they can sometimes become distracted if their environment isn't conducive to sleep. At night it's beneficial to use room-darkening curtains to keep any light from creeping in. Water signs like to sleep in complete darkness, and may even find it difficult to sleep if their room isn't pitch black. Using blackout shades and dark heavy curtains will help make your bedroom cozy and dark, just the way water signs like it. Alternatively, you may consider using a sleeping mask to prevent any light from bothering you while you sleep.

Get Cozy

There's nothing quite like taking a long bath or shower and then snuggling up in a thick bath towel. For water signs self-care means pampering yourself with luxury whenever you can. A simple way to do this is to invest in high-quality towels or a robe that you can wear after you've washed away any negative emotions from the day. The soft, fluffy material will help you feel safe and protected. If you have the opportunity, consider buying a towel warmer as well.

Go It Alone

When it comes to sports and leisure, water signs tend to do best with activities that take place outside and don't involve a lot of people. This means that team sports aren't always the best option for you. Water signs should avoid recreational leagues that attract a lot of people. Instead, they do better with low-pressure activities that focus on nature, such as walking, hiking, and climbing. You may find that you, as a water sign, don't really like competition, and there's absolutely nothing wrong with that.

Find an activity out in nature that suits you best. If you feel like you want some company, invite a few trusted friends along to join you.

Enjoy a Cheesy Indulgence

Dairy is Cancer-ruled, so take full advantage with a cheesy treat! Beyond the typical cheese platter, you can celebrate your love of this dairy delight with a slice of cheesecake, some oh-so-classy caprese, or a bowl of baked mac and cheese. The possibilities are endless.

Still not cheesy enough? Take a cheese-making class! After all, sharing her love for something with others is a dream come true for Cancer. You may even develop a friendship or two along the way.

Do Nighttime Activities

S ome water signs are morning people, but most thrive in the nighttime hours. That's because the night calls to water signs. It is dark and peaceful, and they often feel that they are protected when the sun is down. If you are feeling vulnerable, plan a nighttime activity, such as stargazing, watching fireworks, or going for a simple drive or walk around your neighborhood with a friend. The key is to take some time to appreciate the quiet and calm that come with the evening hours, allowing the shift from chaotic day to tranquil night to ease your mind.

Treat Yourself to Ice Cream

Watery Cancer isn't just sensitive to emotions— she is also uniquely tuned in to the five senses, especially taste. Ice cream, especially blends with rich flavors such as caramel and dark chocolate, is the perfect pairing of sweet and salty. In need of a pick-me-up? Take yourself out for an ice-cream cone, or better yet, invest in a home ice-cream maker so you can enjoy this treat year round. The cold weather blues will be no match for you this year!

Find Some Privacy

You may have noticed that, as a water sign, you need quiet and privacy to get your work done. When it comes to your job, you will be more productive working in a cubicle or by yourself than in an open-plan office or large group. You tend to get overwhelmed when you have too many people around you, so when you really need to concentrate, try retreating to your own secluded space. This will help keep you away from all the hustle and bustle, and limit your distractions.

When you feel the need to talk to others, a communal kitchen or break room is your ideal space. This is where you can comfortably mingle with coworkers before going back to your cubbyhole to get some work done. If you have a job where a group environment is highly valued, try speaking to your supervisor and letting them know how you work best. You might be surprised by how understanding they will be!

Take a Cruise

From sailing across the Pacific to snorkeling in the tropics, there is no doubt that a cruise is the ultimate vacation. This is especially true for watery Cancer. Symbolized by the Crab, Cancer can't get enough of water—specifically oceans. She doesn't need to be swimming to feel the soothing effects of the salt water: just relaxing beside it or sailing over it is enough. A small ship is preferable to a huge ocean liner, as Cancer desires intimate settings and personal space to get her daily dose of "me time."

Go for a Swim

_____

Being a homebody, Cancer prefers relaxation to exercise (but really, how many people don't?). That said, it is still important for her to get her body moving. An exercise that Cancer may enjoy is swimming. This watery sign can't resist a little H_2O. If you have a pool, you can set up a routine of swimming laps each morning during the warm months. During the colder months (or if you don't own a swimming pool), you can join a gym that has a pool, typically for a low monthly fee.

Drink Alkaline Water

Ruled by the water element and symbolized by the Crab, Cancer requires a lot of water in her self-care routine. And this doesn't end with the water outside of her body. Cancer should be especially mindful of the water she puts into her body as well. Slightly alkaline natural spring or mineral water may be a good option for occasionally mixing up your water intake for Cancerian health.

The term *alkaline* refers to the pH level of the water. The lower the pH level, the more acidic a substance is; the higher the pH level, the less acidic it is. Drinking water with a slightly higher pH level may help neutralize the acid in your body, restoring balance. This is especially helpful if you suffer from acid reflux. Some studies have shown alkaline water is also better at regulating blood flow than more acidic water is, and may help reduce high blood pressure. So drink up!

Visualize a Sailing Adventure

As an emotional sign, Cancer is often full of racing thoughts—some not so helpful. A quick meditation break can be just the thing to relax your nerves and refocus your attention. Take 5-10 minutes to sit in a quiet place. Close your eyes and picture a sailboat on the horizon. As you visualize this image, take deep breaths in and out, feeling any pent-up tension or worry release with each breath. You can also add calm waves to your mental picture, and match your breathing to the rise and fall of these waves.

Seek Out a Sauna or Steam Room

The benefits of a sauna or steam room go far beyond simple stress relief. Sitting in a sauna or steam room can improve your circulation, ease muscle pain, and help with some skin problems. For water signs, taking a sauna is a great way to cleanse the soul and calm the mind. Look to see if a local gym or spa has one you can use. Sit and let the dry heat of the sauna or the hot steam of the steam room surround you and loosen the stress in your body.

If you don't have access to a stream room, you can create your own budget version by turning your shower on hot for a few minutes, shutting the door and windows, and letting the room fill with steam. Sit in a towel and enjoy the sensation of moisture floating all around you!

Get Cooking

Cooking and baking are wonderful outlets for water signs, though when given the choice, they tend to stick to the basics they've already mastered rather than experiment with new recipes. After all, if you have a handful of staple dishes that you know you can create easily and well, why would you want to try something new and risk it tasting terrible? Comfort food in particular appeals to a hungry water sign. Everything from macaroni and cheese to mashed potatoes and pancakes are usually big hits. So, why not keep your experimentation to your preferences, and buy a comfort food cookbook that can help expand your repertoire of recipes?

Take a Beach Vacation

Indulge the innate connection you have to water by taking a vacation near a beach. Being by the water will help recharge your batteries when you are feeling depleted. The warm weather in most popular beach spots is perfect for a water sign who is hoping to lounge on the sand and let their worries fade away.

Look for vacation destinations that also include water activities, such as lessons in paddle boarding or snorkeling, to help you connect with your element. If you can swing an all-inclusive resort, you'll get even more bang for your buck, with food, lodging, entertainment, and drinks included.

Create a "Cocoon"

Cancer is deeply connected to the home. As a deep-feeling sign, she readily gives her all to helping others, but it is important for her to also nurture her own needs. This means plenty of space to be alone. At home Cancer can truly relax and focus on herself, without the worry of hurting anyone's feelings. Create privacy in your home (a personal "cocoon" from external elements) that lets you fully disconnect from the outside world. Use curtains in deep shades to keep out prying eyes and invoke an aura of moonlight. If you have a yard, consider planting trees or adding a simple fence around the perimeter.

Watch a Cereus Bloom

The beautiful cereus flower is not just special due to its appearance. It also boasts a unique quality: it only blooms at night. Just like Cancer, cereus flowers draw power from the moon, opening up in its light while other blossoms (and signs) shine brightest in the sun. Some varieties of the cereus, such as *Selenicereus grandiflorus*, only bloom once each year for a single night! You can purchase your own cereus flower and watch it bloom at night, or take a trip to witness the *Selenicereus* bloom in the wild. The *Selenicereus* can be found in parts of Florida, Mexico, and a number of islands in the Caribbean.

Enjoy Refreshing Melon

Summery, sweet, and watery, melons represent Cancer perfectly. Symbolized by the Crab, Cancer lives for days at the beach, and melons such as cantaloupe and honeydew should be her go-to refreshment to keep cool in the hot months.

Share your summer vibes with friends and family by serving melon with smoked salmon as an appetizer or side to dinner. If you are attending an outdoor gathering, consider slicing up a bunch of different melons for a delicious fruit salad everyone will enjoy.

Take Ice-Skating Lessons

E ven frozen water has a special place in a water sign's heart. Just because you can't see the water moving and hear it lapping doesn't mean it is any less soothing or refreshing! In fact, ice can be invigorating for a water sign. Try embracing your cold side by taking beginners' ice-skating lessons. A number of world-class ice-skaters have been water signs. If you already have had some practice and aren't in the mood for a full lesson, try going to a local skating rink and just skate on your own for a little while. You may find that the smooth cut of the blade over ice soothes you.

Learn Something New

Mentally, water signs can understand a whole concept quickly because they intuitively feel it, rather than logically piece it together. The details are not important to them; all they need is to trust their gut and the emotions they are feeling inside. Their empathy is what helps them understand.

Use this superpower by learning something new—topics like philosophy and religion are a great place for water signs to start. These categories often require your ability to grasp a larger concept and understand things at a holistic level, rather than memorize detailed facts and figures. You may even find it beneficial to watch documentaries or listen to lectures in addition to reading a book—whatever sparks your passion!

Bake a Loaf of Bread

Cancer knows that home is truly where the heart lies. And is there anything more homey than a warm loaf of bread fresh out of the oven? As a nurturing sign, Cancer values family, and the home that brings them all together.

If you are missing loved ones, or simply in need of a little extra comfort, bake some bread. The aroma and steam will fill your kitchen—and your heart—with wholesome, happy feelings. Plus, you'll have a tasty treat to enjoy for the whole week.

Try a Boxing Workout

While water signs don't usually respond well to exercises that require a lot of repetition, a boxing workout is definitely an exception. In fact, a few world champion boxers over the years have been water signs. Boxing workouts are a great emotional and physical release if you've been feeling stressed or angry. The power and strength you'll feel when you learn with an expert to kick, punch, and duck properly will keep you coming back to the gym for more. Initially, you may find it difficult to get used to the new motions, but once your body adapts, boxing training is actually a very fluid activity, perfect for water signs! Look into beginners' classes in your local area.

Take Some Alone Time

As a sign that spends so many hours looking after and caring for others, Cancer needs a wellness routine that allows her to give back to herself. As you plan out your day, make a point to carve out time alone. This can be a time to rest, or time to do a fun activity that is just for you. Whether it is 5 minutes to daydream, or an hour to read a good book, this time to yourself is the perfect way to relax and recharge your batteries.

Decorate Your Home
with Seashells

A s one of the three water signs, and symbolized by the Crab, Cancer has a deep connection to the sea. Even if you live miles and miles away from a body of water, seashells can bring the water to you. Incorporate seashells into your home with a set of shell wind chimes placed near a window, or individual shells arranged along a fireplace mantel or on shelves in your living room.

Seashells also magnetize love. In Greek mythology, the goddess of love, Aphrodite, rose from the sea in a large shell. Placing seashells in your home will invoke the goddess's power to draw new love to you, or keep a current relationship strong.

Cuddle

———

Cuddling isn't just fun—it's also good for your health! Experts say that cuddling (whether with a friend, partner, or family member) releases the feel-good hormone oxytocin. Oxytocin boosts mood levels and also helps to ease physical pain.

As an affectionate sign, Cancer is quite the cuddle pro. If you are feeling a little down in the dumps, or have a muscle or joint ache, put your talent to the test. Additionally, if you sleep alone, consider keeping a body pillow on the bed to stimulate that cozy feeling as you drift off to dreamland.

Buy a Comfy Chair

Home is a safe haven for sensitive Cancer. It is where she goes to refocus and shut off all of the noise of the outside world. Because she spends a lot of time at home, Cancer needs accents that make her space as cozy as possible. These allow her to fully relax and restore her Cancerian energy.

A large circular armchair is the perfect addition to your home sanctuary. As you embrace the comfort of your chair, the rounded arms will make you feel as though you are being hugged back.

Express Your Feelings

_____

You feel so deeply, water sign, it's only natural that sometimes your emotions spill over and become overwhelming. Water signs are often receptive and inwardly focused. While you are very good at recognizing your feelings, you find it difficult to express them to others. You have trouble articulating what's inside. Instead, you would prefer that your loved ones just understand what you are feeling rather than having to explain it to them.

Practice expressing your emotions by keeping a journal. At least once a day, preferably at night after you've spent the day processing emotions, write down how you feel. If you are struggling with where to begin, start with the words *I feel* and go from there. Remember that no one will ever read this journal unless you want them to, so don't feel self-conscious. Just write what feels natural.

Indulge in Rainy Days

———————

Some water signs prefer moody, cool, gray weather to bright sunshine. If you have the opportunity, indulge in a rainy day by staying inside, snuggling up on the couch, and listening to the rain beating down outside. You may choose to read a book or listen to music, whatever feels right. If you are feeling adventurous, you may even want to go for a walk in the rain. Make sure you have the right equipment—every water sign should have a decent raincoat and pair of rain boots. Check the weather forecast often to stay ahead of any potential rainy days.

Invest in Efficient Household Items

Home is Cancer's domain. Here, you have the space and privacy to enjoy all of your favorite activities, such as reading and crafting. It is important that the Cancerian home operates smoothly so you don't need to waste hours on small to-do items that leave you more exhausted than before. Home gadgets such as herb cutters, automatic floor vacuums, and programmable thermostats will save you time, energy, and sometimes money. If there are household tasks getting in the way of your much-needed personal time, you can find dozens of solutions online at affordable prices.

Keep Photo Memories

Scrapbooks, photo albums, and iPhone picture galleries are all treasures to water signs. They love to flip through their favorite memories and reminisce about old times or relive their happiest moments.

Spend time putting together collections of photos that chronicle each part of your life. You can organize them in whatever way feels right to you. The goal is to make sure you are surrounded by your most cherished memories at all times. You may even consider putting together a photo collage that you can frame and hang on the wall. You can indulge your love of photos even further by creating a scrapbook or online photo book for your loved ones on their birthdays. The personal touch will bring tears and smiles.

Treat a Friend

As a compassionate sign, Cancer needs to have a self-care routine that balances out her giving nature. Sometimes, though, the best way to restore your own energy is through making someone else happy. Delight a friend with a simple, humorous present that reminds them of you: crab apple jelly. With dozens of online recipes, you can make your own jelly in just a few easy steps. Divide the jelly into clear jars, add a ribbon, and surprise your friend!

Listen to Classical Music

Cancer loves period music with original instruments. The moving sounds and sophisticated atmosphere of a classical performance delight her keen senses. Bring a loved one along to share the experience with, or go alone to fully immerse yourself and focus on the sights and sounds of the performance. You can also use a pair of opera glasses for a classic touch. For a truly stunning performance, visit a major concert hall, such as Carnegie Hall in New York; Symphony Hall in Boston; or the Sydney Opera House.

Make Water a Part of
Your Sleep Routine

While many water signs don't have trouble falling asleep, you may find that turning on a sound machine that features the sounds of rain, waves, or running water will make you feel more relaxed when you are drifting off to dreamland. Some water signs find that they are distracted by their emotions when they are trying to go to sleep. They replay things that happened throughout the day and relive how those things made them feel instead of quieting their minds. Sound machines can help focus your mind and ward off any distractions. Simply breathe deeply and listen to the sounds around you, and you'll be asleep in no time.

Embrace Your "Crabby" Side

Cancer is symbolized by the Crab. With its hard outer shell and soft interior, the Crab is the perfect representation of this tough yet sensitive water sign. Display your astrological connection with a crab totem. A totem is an object that serves as an emblem for a person or group. This figurine will be a proud symbol of your celestial roots, as well as a reminder to remain strong but never lose your sensitive side. Be sure to place your totem on a mantel or table where you will see it daily.

Stay Grounded

It is important for water signs to live close to water (or visit it as often as possible) as a way of staying grounded. A view of some body of water from your home window will orient you and keep you stable, especially when you are feeling vulnerable or over-whelmed by your emotions. Seeing water can bring balance to your life that you would otherwise miss. The closer you can get to the water, the better. Watch out for high-rise apartments, though, even if they have a great view of water in the distance. Being up high can make water signs feel lost and aimless, as if they have no roots.

Decorate with Ocean Hues

—————————

Your home is a reflection of who you are and what you love. Water signs need a calming and soothing environment to thrive in, and the first way to accomplish this is to surround yourself with colors that are reminiscent of water. Look for muted, cool tones like light blue, gray, and deep green, accented with splashes of vibrant, warm colors like red and orange. You may even want to try painting a mural or pattern that makes you think of water on one of your walls. Above all, your home should be comfortable and familiar to you. Use color to make it your own.

Visit the Past in Style

———————

Cancer is a sign deeply rooted in the romance of the past. In fact, many Cancerians can be found working as historians. Whether it's vintage cars, music, or fashion, you take a special interest in the nostalgia, style, and magic of generations past. Spend an afternoon (or full day if you like!) visiting the past in an aesthetically pleasing way by antique shopping or enjoying a vintage car or fashion show. This quick and sophisticated trip into the past will boost your mood—and maybe teach you something new in the process.

Hone Your Photography Skills

———————————

As a water sign, you have incredible observation skills and an eye for beauty. This makes you the ideal photographer. You are able to identify poignancy in any scene, and isolate it with the perfect shot. You also love to keep copies of all the photographs you take so you can revisit these moments whenever you want.

To enhance your photography skills, consider investing in a high-quality camera with digital capabilities. This way you can have a digital record of your work, in addition to prints. Before you purchase, do some research to find out which camera will be best for you and your skill level.

Make a Pot of Soup

Warm, pleasant...wait, are we talking about soup or Cancer? Both, actually! Cancer appreciates a quality comfort food like soup, especially during the frigid months. In fact, while you thrive in more mild climates, you can turn the coldest day warm and inviting with a big pot of your favorite soup or stew! Try savory flavors like bacon corn chowder, or a seasonal favorite like pumpkin or squash soup. Creamy, mild flavors will appeal to your Cancerian tastes.

Embrace Your Sentimental Side

Whether they are celebrating birthdays, Christmas, or Valentine's Day, water signs love the holidays and any happy occasion. You especially love the sentimentality of tradition. Think about all the ways you can participate in holiday or birthday customs with the people you love. This may mean cooking a special meal for everyone, setting up decorations, or just spending time catching up with family and friends. Use your creative side to start new traditions, and encourage your loved ones to get involved. These rituals will help you feel closer to the people you cherish most.

Decorate with Matching Sets

As an emotional and nurturing sign, Cancer delights in both giving and receiving love. Home accents in doubles and matching pairs attract love to you, while encouraging affection and strong bonds among your current relationships. Matching décor will also maintain balance in your home.

Try pairs or sets of three in deep colors reminiscent of the ocean. Shades such as navy blue and teal have a calming effect that will promote relaxation in your home. Great accents to purchase in doubles include candlesticks for your dining room table, lounge chairs for your living room, and nightstands for your bedroom.

Buy an Aquarium

Just because you don't live right next to a body of water doesn't mean you can't make the aquatic a part of your everyday life. One of the easiest ways to bring the ocean home is to invest in an aquarium. As a water sign, you'll find solace in the cool blue ripples of the water and the fluid movement of the fish swimming by. It's true that keeping a healthy aquarium does require research, advice from experts, money, and time, but the cost is well worth the benefits you'll see almost instantly in your mood.

Boost Confidence
with Narcissus Oil

Humble and compassionate Cancer is eager to raise others up. Sometimes in this process, however, she may look down to realize that she herself has been sinking. While care for others is important, it is also crucial that Cancer recognize and celebrate her own triumphs and abilities. A great way to give yourself a little confidence boost is with narcissus oil.

In Greek mythology Narcissus was a man so self-absorbed that he fell in love with his own reflection. To teach the importance of striking a balance between humility and self-assurance, the gods turned him into the narcissus flower. The essential oil made from this flower can be diffused. As the fragrance fills the room, you'll feel the oil's healing powers take effect. Be sure to avoid direct contact with the skin, and dilute the oil in water when diffusing.

Volunteer

———————————

In nature inactive water becomes stagnant and attracts bacteria. Water needs to run, gurgle, babble, and sway. Water signs are the same way. Doing nothing can make a water sign feel useless and bored. To quench your desire to be active and helpful, volunteer at an organization that you care about deeply. Play with dogs at a shelter, read to children at the library, or make lunches for the homeless. For you, being active doesn't just mean moving your body; it also means spending your time meaningfully. These small acts can change the world!

Shop at a Flea Market

Take an older friend or family member or two along on a fun outing to a flea market! As a sign rooted in history and "the good ol' days," Cancer will love sifting through the items of years past—especially when she spots something from her own childhood. She will also enjoy listening to an older companion reminisce about their own childhood and the items that may be foreign to her but spark dear memories for them.

Join a Club

———————

Water signs love to be included in groups, even though they can sometimes get overwhelmed by too many people. The sense of belonging is important for them to feel appreciated and loved. The key for you as a water sign is to find a small group that focuses on something you really love. This could be a book club that meets once a month, a cooking class, or a wildlife club that goes on adventures in nature. There will be no shortage of interesting conversation; you'll find loads to talk about with people who share your loves.

Get Busy

Cancer, as an emotional sign, can be prone to overactive thoughts and feelings of melancholy. Sometimes the best way to beat stress or the blues is to find a project that keeps your mind and body busy. Tasks you can do around the house include organizing your closet, clearing out old emails on your computer, and cleaning those spaces that you haven't had time to maintain lately. These projects won't only clear your mind, but will also give you a sense of taking charge of your life, even in those chaotic phases when it seems like everything is out of your hands.

Go Scuba Diving

In need of a little rejuvenation? Tap into your natural Cancerian element with a scuba diving adventure. Scuba diving blends Cancer's love of water with her deep sense of curiosity. This revitalizing dip in the water is the perfect way to get your blood flowing if you have felt a bit sluggish recently, or recharge your batteries when you are burnt out. Start a recommended scuba diving course, and get your scuba diving certificate. You may even spot a few of your astrological kin (the crab) during the dive!

Start a Collection

Since water signs feel at home near bodies of water, it makes sense for them to pick up pieces of those water sources with them wherever they go. Start collecting stones, rocks, or shells from every body of water you visit. The energy of the water will stay within these objects and help keep you balanced when you are on dry land. When you are feeling lost, sit quietly and hold each object in your hands. Feel the positive vibrations radiating from them. If you'd like, you can create an altar of your water objects in your bedroom to help attract calm thoughts while you drift off to dreamland. Or, when you are in need of an energy boost, put one in your purse or pocket so you can hold it whenever you want as you go about your day.

Draw

Sensitive Cancer is a visual sign. She often needs to see a picture laid out in front of her to understand the full idea, but once she does, she can spot details no one else noticed. Imagery can also enable her to express and reflect on her thoughts and feelings far better than words ever could.

Embrace your inner artist and release your emotions by drawing. Don't think; just let your pencil or pen guide you. Consider bringing a small sketchbook wherever you go so you can draw whenever the urge strikes.

Don't Go to the Desert

Dry climates don't suit water signs well. You need to feel moisture in the air in order to breathe easy. While it's not advisable for water signs to live in a dry climate like the desert, if you do, there are certain things you can try to keep the air around you moist. The easiest is to research and purchase a humidifier for your home and run it as needed. This will significantly improve the quality of the air.

You can also look for an essential oil diffuser that uses water, which not only adds moisture to the air, but also diffuses essential oils to impact your mood. Experiment with different scents to find the one that is right for you.

Create Your Own Water Feature

Running water is soothing to water signs at work and at home. Purchase a small water fountain that you can keep near your desk at work to help you through stressful moments. When you are feeling overwhelmed, take a few moments to focus on the sound of the water and nothing else. You can leave the fountain running all day to help keep you feeling balanced and calm. If you have space at home, purchase another water fountain for your living room, or wherever you spend the most time. The trickling water will keep you company whenever you need it.

Spending time outdoors is also beneficial for water signs, so look for a water fountain that can be set up on a deck or in your backyard.

Visit the Galápagos Islands

B eautiful views, seclusion from the rest of the world, and the perfect blend of adventure and relaxation—is there any location more perfect for Cancer? Probably not. But this isn't your typical tropical vacation: the Galápagos Islands are a special destination every Cancer should journey to at least once.

The historical roots of these islands will especially delight Cancer. From the inspiration for Charles Darwin's theories on evolution to the adventures of sea pirates, the Galápagos hold countless stories of the world. The Galápagos also have a feature that Cancer will have a special connection to: the Sally Lightfoot crab. Common in the Galápagos, this crustacean (and astrological symbol for Cancer) has a beautiful orange and red shell with striking blue accents.

Add a Little Heat

Feeling a bit lethargic? No worries! You can jump-start your motivation with a bit of heat. Inserting just a short burst of controlled heat to your day will balance out your water element without overpowering it. Heat and movement stimulate blood flow, which increases the release of feel-good hormones, such as endorphins, dopamine, and serotonin. Doing a vigorous exercise or diffusing a stronger scent like cinnamon essential oil (just be sure to dilute it in a lot of water to keep the heat at a manageable level!) are great ways to clear out stagnant energy. Try adding a little cinnamon to your morning tea or coffee, attending a hot yoga class, or diffusing a diluted ginger essential oil.

Write a Story

_____

Your imagination is expansive as a water sign. You have the gift of creation, seamlessly moving between reality and the made-up worlds in your mind. Some of the best writers working today are water signs, so try putting your visions down on paper and sharing them with the world. Start small by writing a short story, or even just the beginning paragraphs of a larger project. Live inside your own imagination for a while and see what comes forth. Remember that not every sentence you write needs to be perfect. Just focus on expressing your ideas, and you can go back and revise what you've already written later on.

Keep a Dream Diary

Water signs have notoriously vivid dreams that stick with them after waking. You may even dream of future events, or have trouble deciphering if what happened was a dream or reality.

Try keeping a dream diary to chronicle all of the dreams you remember. When you wake up and the dream is fresh in your mind, take a few minutes to write down key words that describe the dream. Ask yourself some questions: How did you feel? Who was there? What was happening? The more detail you can put on paper, the better able you'll be to interpret the dreams later on.

Find Balance with Selenite

Connect with your celestial ruler, the Moon, with the powers of selenite. Long, slender, and semitranslucent white in color, this crystal is named after Selene, the Greek goddess of the Moon. Like its namesake, selenite represents fertility and nurturing, which are also qualities of Cancer.

Selenite also regulates the flow of both mental and physical energy. As a neutral stone, it does not hold negative energy, nor does it stimulate enthusiasm or movement. Because of this, selenite is the perfect crystal for promoting balance of the mind, body, and spirit. Place this crystal in a central location in your home, or use it in meditation to draw both balance and lunar abundance to you.

Cherish Family Heirlooms

Family is very important to you as a water sign. You take comfort in the familial connections you have, and take pride in your loyalty to family no matter what. Because of this, your bond to your family only grows stronger day by day.

Every family is unique and has their own collection of heirlooms that are passed down from generation to generation. Display your own family heirlooms proudly. They are a special link to your ancestors and show off who you truly are.

Surround Yourself
with Succulents

Succulents are some of the easiest plants to care for—some can grow well in indoor environments and require less frequent watering. These are the perfect plants for a busy water sign. Jade is a particularly popular choice—it is known as the lucky tree, or the money tree, and needs very little care to thrive. The color of the flowers that bloom from the plant can be either pink or white. Not only are succulents beautiful to look at, but surrounding yourself with green is a great way to reduce stress and create a calming, nurturing environment. Succulents can also increase productivity and concentration, so consider placing one near your workstation as well.

Adorn Yourself with Silver

Silver is reminiscent of the Moon, Cancer's ruling body. Like the moon, silver is a reflective material, but its connection to Cancer's celestial ruler extends far beyond outward appearance. Silver is a healing element that is believed to enhance the powers of the lunar cycle, particularly the full and new moon. Wearing silver will help Cancer sync her emotions to the moon's phases, and manage the thoughts and feelings that are most prominent during the full and new moon. Additionally, just as the moon reflects light, silver reflects negativity away from you.

As a sensitive sign, you can easily feel overwhelmed by the noisy world around you, as well as your own over-active mind. Wearing a silver necklace or earrings will help you redirect negative energy away from your life.

Show Yourself

Let out the real you. Cancer has strong bonds and relationships with her friends and family members. However, she can also hide behind a tough outer shell, refusing to let others see her vulnerable side for fear of getting hurt. Practice letting people in and showing them the real, wonderful you. If it helps, you can come up with a question or empowering statement to ask or say to yourself in times when you feel yourself retreating into your shell. Try asking yourself, "How would I react in this situation if I were not afraid?"

Just admitting that you have certain fears can be enough motivation to face them head-on. Remember this: true friends and family members love you for who you really are.

Skip the Spicy Foods

Water signs can be picky when it comes to their diet and nutrition. For example, they usually don't like spicy food and tend to stick to more muted cuisines, with the exception of salami and cured meats. The salty taste of these treats appeals to them. In fact, you may find you have more cravings for salty foods than sweet foods. That's not to say you don't like something sweet every now and again. A small piece of candy or baked good is all you need. Water signs also love carbs and will never pass up a piece of pizza when offered, though they are partial to pizza with meat toppings instead of vegetable toppings. So listen to your body, skip the spicy, and choose the foods that most appeal to your taste buds *and* your nutritional needs. Bon appétit!

Ask for Help

Cancer is the most nurturing of the zodiac signs. She gives and gives, and asks for nothing in return. Over time, friends and family members come to expect that she is never in need of assistance. This isn't because they are selfish or uncaring—they just can't remember the last time they heard Cancer ask for help. Practice asking for that assistance when you need it. It is not a sign of weakness, and you are not putting people out when you ask them to help you. For all of the support you give them, they are more than happy to reciprocate, so let them!

Protect Yourself from Energy Vampires

Water signs feel deeply and can easily be drained by emotionally manipulative people. Trust your gut when it comes to whom you spend your time with. If you find that someone is particularly toxic to you or you feel that your energy is depleted after seeing them, consider removing them from your life. As a water sign, you need to care for your emotional wellness and protect yourself against energy vampires. If you are feeling particularly vulnerable, try carrying around a piece of rose quartz to buffer against negativity. Wearing the crystal as a necklace near your heart is even better.

Host a House "Warming"

Home is Cancer's sanctuary, and her loved ones are her lifeblood. If you have been feeling a little down in the dumps lately, warm up your home with the love and laughter of friends and family by hosting a house "warming" party.

As a nurturing sign, Cancer is also the perfect host or hostess, and she delights in zipping around her kitchen and living spaces with plates of food, napkins for spills, and great story anecdotes. The fun and love you share will be the perfect reward for your preparation.

Stay Away from Strong Scents

———————

Have you ever noticed that you are very sensitive to scents and often get headaches or feel nauseated when you are around heavy perfumes or colognes? Water signs have a very keen sense of smell, which can be a superpower, but also a hindrance at times. To avoid being overloaded with an offending smell, it's best for you to avoid sharing elevators or enclosed spaces with anyone wearing a heavy scent. It will stick to your clothes and linger around you all day. You should especially stay away from the perfume section in any department stores!

Revel in the Full Moon

Celebrate the height of your celestial ruler with a full moon ritual. One great way to show your appreciation for the moon and its powerful gifts is to create an altar. Use this space to burn candles and arrange crystals, personal tokens, or whatever else honors the energies of the moon.

You can also burn some ceremonial sage (not the type found in the spice aisle at grocery stores) in a fireproof bowl at your altar. Sage has been used for centuries in spiritual and healing practices. The floral scents evoke feminine power and expel negative energy.

Tidy up any obvious clutter and open as many doors and windows as possible in your home. Place the sage in a fireproof bowl and light the stick. Blow out the sage, and use the fireproof bowl to hold the smoking stick as you spread the smoke around the room in order to draw out any negativity.

Flavor Your Water

———

You already know that drinking enough water is one key to good health, but this is especially true for water signs. You need to ingest enough water every day to keep your body strong. Staying hydrated doesn't have to be boring, though. Hydrating with water is by far the best option, but you can spice things up by adding a few ingredients to make your own flavored water. Try stirring in a few strawberries or raspberries, or just add a splash of lemon juice or cucumbers to your water pitcher. Not only do these ingredients brighten the flavor of your water, but many of them have antioxidant properties that can boost your immune system.

Hire a Cleaning Service

Cancer spends much of her time at home, enjoying solitary activities and a lot of rest to keep her batteries fully charged. As a sensitive sign, she is also keenly aware of messy spaces, and this disorder in her home can leave her feeling overwhelmed or unmotivated. Invest in a service that does a complete deep clean of your home once a week, or once every few weeks, to avoid unnecessary stress. Just like you, your home deserves to be well taken care of.

Meditate Alone

Spiritual practices such as meditation are best done alone for water signs. That's because meditation is a time of emotional vulnerability, and water signs are highly sensitive to other people's energies. If you are meditating with a group, you may inadvertently absorb other people's feelings rather than focus on your own. Instead, find a comfortable, private area where you can let your guard down and feel safe. Make sure your meditation spot is relaxing and inviting, with a soft seat and soothing ambiance. It may help to listen to quiet music or put on a sound machine to keep you focused.

Explore Your Ancestry

Cancer is a sign deeply rooted to the past. A highly intuitive, and many would say psychic, zodiac sign, she has a connection to the subconscious of all things. Explore the history of your family and the past people who helped shape you by digging into your ancestry. Ask family members about their own childhoods, and the relatives who came before them. What were these distant relatives like? What did they do for a living? And how did they impact the lives and values of your current family?

There are also many ancestry websites and digitalized records available to fill in gaps that living relatives cannot. What you learn can help you better understand not only your roots, but also yourself and your place in the world.

Sort Through Your Mementos

As a nostalgic sign, Cancer likes to keep mementos and souvenirs, which can pile up over time. Take a few hours, or a day, to go through your collection. Sort out what matters most and is worth keeping, versus what is taking up space and can be let go. The trip down memory lane will lift your spirits, while the act of cleansing your space of clutter will free up room for things that are more important.

Get a Worry Doll

Ruled by the Moon, Cancer is a nurturing sign who tries her best to help everyone and maintain peace. But, sometimes, this urge to fix everyone's troubles can lead to a buildup of anxious thoughts. Use a worry doll to soothe your worries.

A tradition of the Mayan civilization, worry dolls originated as dolls that children kept under their pillows to protect against nightmares. These dolls absorb the concerns of the user, so they can sleep (or go about their day) worry-free. Keep a worry doll under your pillow, or carry it in your pocket to ease stressful thoughts.

Chase Your Wanderlust

Sticking close to home is a comfort for many water signs. It's okay to prefer staying in to going out, but you should try to challenge your homebody habit by booking a trip somewhere far away every now and again. You may initially feel anxious about being away from home, but the excitement of seeing far-off, different lands may outweigh the discomfort. The good news is, as long as the room you stay in while traveling is comfortable, you'll be able to feel safe. Water signs just need a secure place to rest their heads, and they'll be able to enjoy new places without too much worry.

Read Poetry

Poetry has a unique way of capturing and channeling emotions. As a sensitive water sign, Cancer has a lot of emotions moving through her at all times, and taking some time to read poetry is a therapeutic act of self-care. The best poems for Cancer are those written from the raw emotion and honest experiences of the author. Talented writers who are particularly well-known for their passionate, uncompromising poems include Sylvia Plath, E.E. Cummings, and Emily Dickinson.

Adopt a Dog or Cat

The world is broken up into dog people and cat people. While there are many people who enjoy both types of domesticated animals, they usually have a preference for one over the other. Water signs are definitely more cat people, but have been known to fall in love with small dogs as well.

Cats are independent and curious, traits that water signs appreciate. Small dogs can be outgoing and rambunctious (depending on their breed), also characteristics that appeal to a sometimes moody water sign. The key for water signs is finding a small animal to share your space with, one that fits well into the home you've already created for yourself. Just make sure to get expert advice on adopting (and properly caring for) your chosen pet from a local animal shelter before you commit.

Celebrate the Summer Solstice

The sun enters Cancer on the summer solstice, the longest day of the year. Have a celebration in honor of your birth season by throwing a summer solstice party. Cancer knows how to host a memorable affair, and friends and family members alike will delight in your knack for good food, inviting décor, and thoughtful conversation. You can bring elements of both the sun and your astrological sign into play with sun-shaped cookies, beachy accents, and tasty crab cake appetizers.

Go for a Past-Life Reading

Cancer is deeply linked to the subconscious—not just her own, but also those of the people and even events around her. Have a past-life reading done by a psychic. During the reading, they will tap into the times and bodies that you may have existed in before now, drawing a connection between the present you and your past selves. This reading can provide a deeper understanding of your current life, from your values and personality traits, to the experiences you have undergone. Do some research and ask for local recommendations from a trusted source.

Spend Time with Loved Ones

E ven though water signs are homebodies, they do like to socialize when the environment is just right. This usually means hanging out with a small group of close family members or friends. Water signs need to be surrounded by people they trust to feel comfortable enough to kick back and relax.

If you aren't in the mood to venture out beyond your front door, consider inviting your friends or family over for a small dinner party where you can all enjoy one another's company and speak candidly about your thoughts and emotions. This is a water sign's dream get-together!

Send a Thank-You Note to a Mother

Cancer is ruled by the Moon, which represents motherhood and nurturing instincts. Because of this, Cancer has a strong connection with her mom or other motherly figures. Show your appreciation for a mother figure in your life by writing a thank-you note. Whether she is your own mother, a friend who has a child, or a woman who showed you motherly care and guidance, she will be moved by your simple message. It may be just the inspiration she needs to get through a tough time or remember that she is doing a wonderful job.

Take a Milk Bath

Given Cancer's connection to nurturance and motherhood, it is no surprise that the perfect self-care routine for her involves milk. Channel your inner Cleopatra and indulge in a luxurious ritual she was infamous for: the milk bath.

Many spas allow you to soak in milk- and floral-infused water, or relax as milk is used in massage or other body treatments for your skin. You can also perform this self-care ritual at home by adding one of the many bath products that contain milk (such as bath bombs or soaks) to your bath water.

Take In a Concert

———————

Live music is invigorating for many water signs. While being in crowds can sometimes be overwhelming for them, the positive energy of the music can help them overcome that discomfort. There's nothing quite like singing along to one of your favorite songs live. Surrender to the spirit of the music and let it permeate your being.

If you have the opportunity, look for an outdoor concert where you can combine your love of nature with the power of live music. During the summer months you'll find outdoor music festivals popping up all over the world that attract a variety of artists and fans. Find one that speaks to your unique musical taste!

Try Hydrotherapy

As the first water sign of the zodiac, Cancer needs plenty of H_2O in her self-care regimen. Ease into your natural element with hydrotherapy. This soothing practice can involve a number of treatments, from underwater massages to soaking tubs full of minerals. Hydrotherapy is also a great tool for exercising your body following an operation or injury. Ask your doctor and research the best practices for you and your health needs. You can find a spa near you that offers the many healing effects of hydrotherapy, or create your own therapeutic oasis with a relaxing bath or foot soak.

Attend the Ballet or Opera

As a water sign, you are driven by emotion and feeling. This is why you may feel such an inherent draw toward the performing arts, like dance and theater. Indulge this love by attending a ballet or opera performance in your area. Ballet is a beautiful example of the fluidity of motion, which speaks to water signs on a visceral level, and opera presents a vivid story through the power of song and language. Attending the opera can be a very emotional experience for the audience, so bring your tissues, water sign!

Embrace Your Love of History

Water signs love to travel to different times in their imaginations—that's why historical fiction is the perfect genre for this literary sign. Why not turn that love of different time periods into an excuse to actually visit those historical sites?

Make a list of sites that you have always wanted to see, and start visiting. Studying history requires that you imagine yourself in the same situations as the people of that time. As a water sign, you are incredibly empathetic and understanding, so this skill probably comes easily to you. Use it to your advantage and relive some of the most important moments in history with your own eyes.

Try Probiotics

Cancer rules the stomach, so it is especially important that her self-care routine include practices that manage any stomach upset and keep the digestive system running smoothly. Probiotics help with digestion by stimulating the nerves that control gut movement and balancing the good and bad bacteria in your body. Conditions that probiotics may help with include irritable bowel syndrome, inflammatory bowel disease, and upset caused by antibiotics. Apart from supplements, you can also find probiotics in certain foods, including yogurt, certain cheeses, and pickles. If you are suffering from any health conditions, check with your doctor first.

Catch Frogs

Water, a bit of whimsy...what more could Cancer ask for? As the astrological caretaker, this sign needs self-care practices that allow her to let loose once in a while and invite her inner child out to play. Catching frogs (or attempting to) is the perfect afternoon activity for Cancer to unwind with. Try picking a rainy day to go frog-catching (the rain will draw them out and also appeal to your natural element) at a local pond or marsh. You can also bring along a friend for even more fun and fond memories to look back on.

Trust Your Intuition

Do you sometimes find that you intuitively know what time it is without even checking your watch or phone? That's because water signs have a great internal sense of time. You're probably always early to your appointments, and don't even need to set an alarm to wake up in the morning.

Learn to trust your intuition more in all parts of your life, not just when it comes to being on time. As a water sign, you can usually trust your gut instinct. You have a talent for reading situations and people through how you feel. This is a strength that you can rely on. Don't second-guess yourself so much—learn to listen to that voice in your mind. It's usually right!

Up Your Omega-3s

As a sensitive sign, Cancer is prone to having dozens of different thoughts and feelings running through her at once. This can lead to periods of anxiety or low spirits. Omega-3s can combat these emotions, and are also good for your overall health. Fatty acids like omega-3s serve as energy for your muscles, heart, and other organs, and also as the building blocks for your cells. Ask your doctor (who is familiar with your health and medications) about supplements. You can also find omega-3s in certain foods, such as fatty fish (try mackerel or salmon) and walnuts.

Go to Therapy

While water signs have a lot of emotions swirling around inside, classic therapy might not work for them. They don't like to get stuck living in the past, mulling over things that have already happened. To them, the past is a bottomless well of memory. When it comes to talking about their feelings, they prefer to focus on targeted problems. However, they can certainly benefit from the journey.

If you are considering therapy, ask your doctor for recommendations, and then look around for a therapist who understands exactly what you are looking to get out of your sessions. It may take some trial and error, but eventually you'll find the right professional and right approach for you.

Add Some Anchovies

While some may turn away from this ingredient, Cancer loves the salt and texture anchovies add to a dish. Found at most grocery stores, these small fish resonate with Cancer's natural element, connecting her to her love of the sea and everything in it. Add a few anchovies to your slice of pizza! The flavors of the fish are a perfect complement to the cheese and crust.

But why stop there? You can toss anchovies into a salad, mix them into spaghetti, or serve them over garlic and cheese toast. However you enjoy them, be sure to savor every bite as a reminder of your ocean ties.

Depend on Your Water Friends

Sometimes, in order to really work through a problem, you need to turn to someone who just intuitively understands you. For water signs this means seeking out other water signs. They are usually just as good at listening as you are, and can help you work through whatever is going on in your life at the time. Since water signs are so sympathetic, they will always be around to lend an ear when you need it. It is important for water signs to support one another, especially when it comes to their emotional health and balance.

Set a Good Example

As a nurturing sign, Cancer enjoys being a strong example for her friends and family members. Be a good role model when it comes to your health, both mental and physical, so that your loved ones can learn from you. These exemplary acts can be as simple as getting a good night's sleep or minding your alcohol intake, or as involved as working toward a fitness goal. Watching those you care about follow your lead will be a rewarding experience.

Chant Your Way to Calm

As a water sign, you may become easily over-whelmed by a lot of noise, but chanting may have the reverse effect on you if you are looking to relax and zen out. For centuries Buddhist monks have used chanting as a way to prepare the mind for meditation. You, too, can use this ritual to find peace. Repetitive chanting often mimics the ebb and flow of water, something that innately pleases water signs. Try researching a few chants that you can use in the comfort of your own home. When you are ready to meditate, start chanting, and repeat the words over and over again until a sense of calm sweeps over you.

Meditate with Crystals

Employing the help of the right crystal at the right time can do wonders for balancing your energy and emotions. Look for crystals that are reminiscent of the ocean, such as blue lace agate, aquamarine, and lapis lazuli. Blue lace agate can calm anxiety and worry, aquamarine promotes courage and communication, and lapis lazuli can help you discover the truth about yourself and your life. When you are meditating, hold the crystal of your choosing in your hand or close to your heart. Use its energy and power to achieve your goals, no matter what they are.

Explore Your Artistic Side

Water signs are instinctively very artistic. Tap into your creative side by trying a new craft, such as watercolor painting. Watercolors are a more forgiving medium for novice painters than oil paints. Try painting ocean scenes, waterfalls, or lakes. The act of painting can be very soothing for the artist. If you are struggling at first, you may find it helps to look at an image to replicate as you paint, or purchase an acrylic paint-by-numbers kit. Once you've gotten the hang of brushstrokes and color blending, you can create an original piece.

Practice a Bedtime Meditation

As a sensitive and reflective sign of the zodiac, Cancer often has dozens of thoughts racing through her mind at once. This can sometimes make winding down for sleep at the end of the day a bit of a challenge. One simple way to get your mind ready for bed is with a bedtime meditation. A bedtime meditation is an easy way to channel the stress you've built up from the day and ease your mind into sleep so you are recharged and ready for whatever tomorrow brings.

To do a meditation before bed, simply sit in the lotus position on or beside your bed and close your eyes. Now, picture a calming image or recite a soothing phrase to yourself. Focus on channeling that sense of peace from your mind down to your arms, fingers, legs, and feet. Take note of how your body loosens with each passing moment. Once you feel fully relaxed, you're ready for sleep.

Show Off Another Time Period

If you love a particular historical period, consider decorating part of your home with objects from that era. Because of their empathetic abilities, water signs are able to build worlds in their minds that they can visit every now and again. Bridge the gap between your reality and imagination by surrounding yourself with objects that remind you of another time and place. You could create an American Civil War room, an ancient Egyptian room, or a Viking room.

If you are more in love with a certain place than a time period, apply the same principle. Collect objects from that area and put them on display.

Pamper Yourself

Pampering yourself is essential for any self-care routine. For water signs this means spending time focusing on their outer appearance as well as their inner wellness. Dedicate time to indulging yourself with a spa facial. Facials are great for increasing circulation in your facial muscles and hydrating the skin. They can also decrease puffiness and slow the formation of wrinkles.

If you don't have the budget to pay for a spa-level facial, you can always try at-home masks. Many of these masks are made from ingredients that are already in your pantry or refrigerator, such as cucumber. Research which kind of mask will work best for your skin type.

About the Author

Constance Stellas is an astrologer of Greek heritage with more than twenty-five years of experience. She primarily practices in New York City and counsels a variety of clients, including business CEOs, artists, and scholars. She has been interviewed by *The New York Times*, *Marie Claire*, and *Working Woman*, and has appeared on several New York TV morning shows, featuring regularly on Sirius XM and other national radio programs as well. Constance is the astrologer for *HuffPost* and a regular contributor to Thrive Global. She is also the author of several titles, including *The Astrology Gift Guide*, *Advanced Astrology for Life*, *The Everything® Sex Signs Book*, and the graphic novel series Tree of Keys, as well as coauthor of *The Hidden Power of Everyday Things*. Learn more about Constance at her website, ConstanceStellas.com, or on *Twitter* (@Stellastarguide).